# CULTIVATE RESOURCES

Diane Lindsey Reeves

21st Century Junior Library

Published in the United States of America by:

## CHERRY LAKE PRESS
2395 South Huron Parkway, Suite 200, Ann Arbor, Michigan 48104
www.cherrylakepress.com

Reading Adviser: Beth Walker Gambro, MS, Ed., Reading Consultant, Yorkville, IL

Photo Credits: © Kuznetsov Dmitriy/Shutterstock, cover; © Oleksii Sidorov/Shutterstock, 5; © PintoArt/ Shutterstock, 6; © kelvn/Shutterstock, 7; © PeopleImages.com - Yuri A/Shutterstock, 8–9; © Andri wahyudi/ Shutterstock, 10–11; © GBJSTOCK/Shutterstock, 13; © Zoteva/Shutterstock, 14; © Jacob Lund/Shutterstock, 16; International Fund for Animal Welfare/Pexels.com

**Cherry Lake Press** is an imprint of Cherry Lake Publishing Group.

Library of Congress Cataloging-in-Publication Data has been filed and is available at catalog.loc.gov.

Cherry Lake Publishing Group would like to acknowledge the work of the Partnership for 21st Century Learning, a Network of Battelle for Kids. Please visit Battelle for Kids online for more information.

Printed in the United States of America

Note from publisher: Websites change regularly, and their future contents are outside of our control. Supervise children when conducting any recommended online searches for extended learning opportunities.

# CONTENTS

# DISCOVER THE CULTIVATING RESOURCES CAREER CLUSTER

Start with an interest in nature. Mix in a desire to protect the **environment**. Then add a big dose of Science, Technology, Engineering, and Math (STEM) skills. These ingredients come together in many Cultivating Resources careers from the National Career Clusters® Framework.

Do you like being in nature? Then maybe a Cultivating Resources career is for you!

Some of these careers work with farms. They work with growing food. They work with **livestock** and other animals. Some of these careers work with energy. This energy powers our homes. It powers our cars. It powers our cities and places of work.

Many Cultivating Resources careers work with animals. You can find one that fits you best.

# Look!

Look around your community to see if you can find Cultivating Resources workplaces. Are there any farms? Do you see any signs of solar or wind energy?

Energy takes natural resources. Some of these careers work with those natural resources. Finding clean energy sources is hard. Making better use of natural resources is a concern. There is also the day-to-day need to keep public **utilities** going.

Farmers use science to make sure their soil and their plants stay healthy.

STEM skills are needed in many careers in this cluster. Food, water, and animal careers involve a lot of science. Technology and engineering play roles in environmental and energy-related jobs. Sometimes a college degree is needed. Sometimes special training or experience is needed.

Let's explore the two Cultivating Resources career areas:

- Agriculture
- Energy and Natural Resources

# Create!

Pretend you are a scientist. Your job is to create a new way to fuel cars. Most cars run on gasoline. Electric cars are getting more popular. What other ideas do you have? Draw a picture to show your idea.

# EXPLORE CULTIVATING RESOURCES CAREERS

To **cultivate** something means to **nurture** it and help it grow. That is the idea behind the Cultivating Resources career cluster. It is about nurturing our food sources, water, and animals. It is about helping our forests and wildlife grow in healthy ways. It is about caring for Earth and finding better ways to power it with energy.

Do you enjoy helping things grow? You may like a career in agriculture or forestry.

Agriculture covers all the careers needed to provide our food and water. It involves taking care of animals, plants, and forests. This includes careers like farmers and veterinarians.

Agriculture also includes some surprising choices. Do you know what game wardens do to protect wildlife? Have you heard of **agronomists**? They work hard to grow and improve the crops used in many of our foods.

Energy and **natural resources** cover a wide range of careers. Some careers, like natural resource specialist, focus on improving use of our natural resources. Others, like environmental engineer, focus on creating new **sustainable** energy sources.

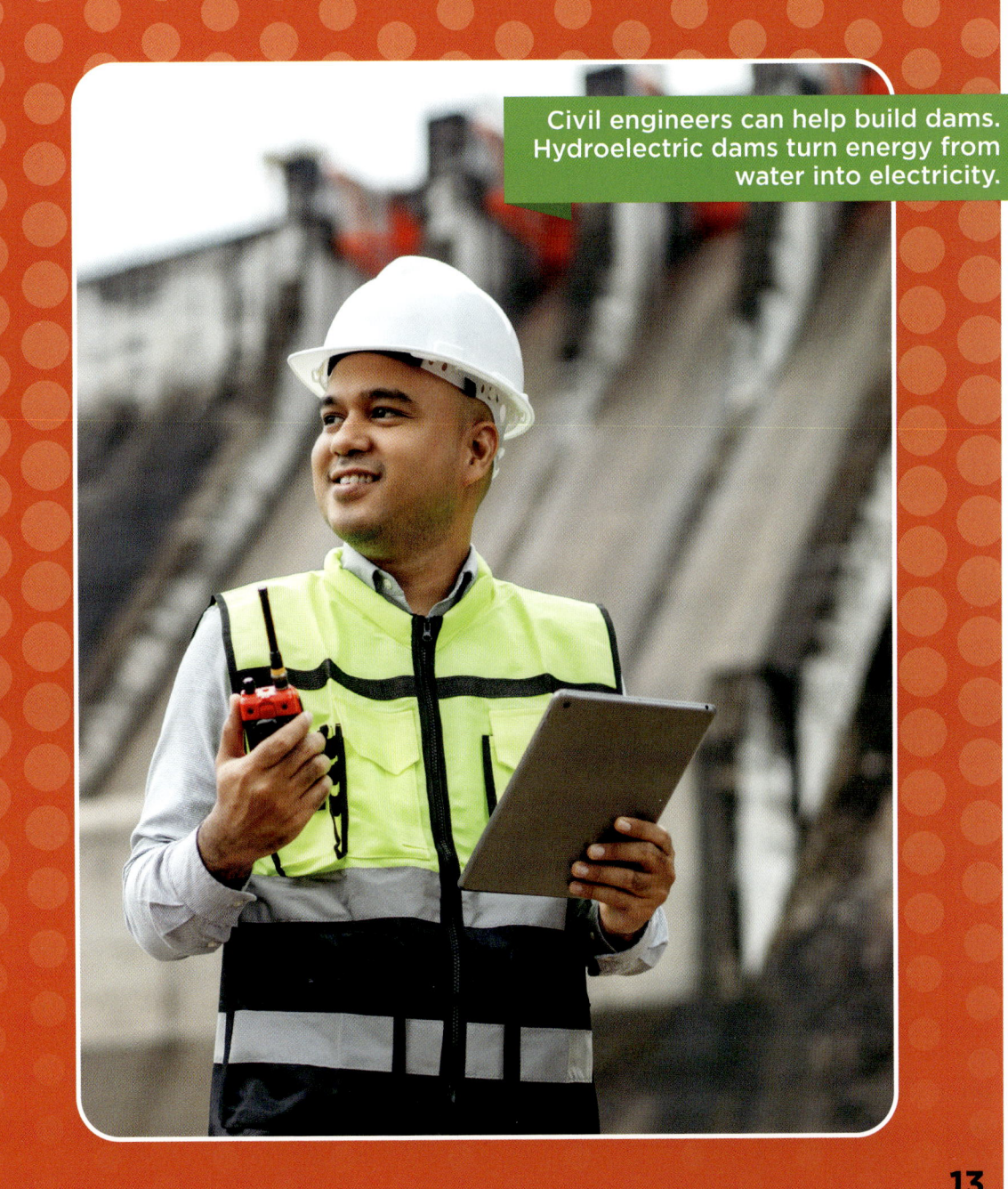

Civil engineers can help build dams. Hydroelectric dams turn energy from water into electricity.

Electrical engineers, linemen, and electricians are just a few careers related to electricity.

14

Careers related to electricity and other public utilities are also included. Examples include line technicians who restore electricity after a bad storm. They also include power grid engineers who design and run power plants.

Would you like to nurture and grow a better world? Consider a career in the Cultivating Resources career cluster.

## Make a Guess!

Can you guess what natural resources are used to light and heat our homes? Ask an adult to help you find answers online. Look for natural resources used in public utilities.

Taking care of the Earth is an important job. Does it seem like something you'd want to do?

# IS CULTIVATING RESOURCES IN YOUR FUTURE?

Do you like animals? Do you like working outdoors? Are you interested in protecting Earth? If your answer is yes, that's your first clue! Cultivating Resources careers might be a good choice for you.

There is no rush to decide. But it can be fun to check out the options. Figure out what you like to do. Think of what you want to know more about.

These clues will help narrow down your choices. Learning about yourself and exploring different careers are good ways to be a career-ready kid.

You can experiment with career ideas, too. Ask an adult to help you talk to someone with a career that interests you. An adult can help you visit places where these people work. Think about what the work is like. Imagine the kinds of problems you can solve.

Being a career-ready kid **motivates** you to do your best work now. You can build a bridge from learning in school to preparing for your future career.

# Think!

Think about the type of Cultivating Resources career that might be a good fit for you. Does it involve working with animals? What about working with alternative energy sources?

Does working at an animal rescue sound like something you'd be good at?

# INVESTIGATE CULTIVATING RESOURCES CAREERS

## Utilities Management
- oil rig operator
- public utility manager
- solar or wind technician
- wastewater collection manager

## Animal Welfare
- animal nutritionist
- wildlife manager
- zoologist

## CULTIVATE RESOURCES

## Plant Care
- botanist
- farmer
- landscape architect

## Conservation
- conservationist
- environmental protection officer
- forest ranger
- green entrepreneur

## Earth & Plant Science
- Geographic Information Systems (GIS) technician
- ecologist
- food scientist
- geologist
- hydrologist

# ACTIVITY

**Practice cultivating resources!** In the spring or summer, plant your own garden. Buy some seeds first.

- Find a good spot outside that gets a lot of sunlight. Prepare the soil. Remove weeds and grass. Add fertilizer. Now it's time to plant the seeds!
- Poke your finger a couple of inches down into the soil. Drop a seed into the hole. Fill it back in. Make sure you space the seeds so that each plant will have enough space. Water your plot!
- Check on your plants every day. You may have to protect them from animals! You may have to give them more or less water.

# Ask Questions!

Protecting the environment is an important way to cultivate resources. What things can you do now to help nurture our planet?

# GLOSSARY

**agronomists** (uh-GRAH-nuh-mists) people who grow crops and manage soil health

**cultivate** (KUHL-tuh-vayt) to nurture or grow

**environment** (in-VIYE-ruh-muhnt) all living and non-living things on Earth, including air, water, land, plants, animals, and climate

**livestock** (LIVE-stahk) farm animals raised for use and profit

**motivates** (MOH-tuh-vayts) provides a person with a reason for taking action

**natural resources** (NAA-chuh-ruhl REE-sors-uhz) materials found in nature that can help people in many ways; forests and fresh water are examples

**nurture** (NUHR-chuhr) take good care of something

**sustainable** (suh-STAY-nuh-buhl) describing a resource that can last a long time without running out or harming the environment

**utilities** (yoo-TIH-luh-teez) services like electricity, water, or gas that are provided by a city or region

# FIND OUT MORE

### Books

Brown, Carron. *I Like the Outdoors . . . What Jobs Are There?* Tulsa, OK: Kane Miller, 2020.

Martin, Steve. *I Like Animals . . . What Jobs Are There?* Tulsa, OK: Kane Miller, 2020.

Rossi, Sofia E., and Carlos Canepa. *Jobs of the Future: Imaginative Careers for Forward-Thinking Kids.* Kansas City, MO: Andrews McMeel, 2022.

### Websites

Explore these online resources with an adult.

NASA Climate Kids: Green Careers

Time For Kids: Your Hot Job—Environment & Sustainability

# INDEX

# ABOUT THE AUTHOR

**Diane Lindsey Reeves** writes books to help students of all ages find bright futures. She lives in North Carolina with her husband and a big kooky dog named Honey. She has four of the best grandkids in the world.